Safeguarding Vulnerable Adults Course Book

OTHER PUBLICATIONS IN THE SERIES:

Basic Nutrition (01BN/0116)
Food Hygiene (02FH/0116)
Fire Safety (03FS/0116)
End of Life Care, Death and Bereavement (05DB/0116)
Person-Centred Planning (06PC/0116)
Diabetes (07DD/0116)
Stroke (08SS/0116)
Dementia Care (09DC/0116)
Managing Aggression (10MA/0116)
Mental Health Issues (11MH/0116)
Health and Safety (12HS/0116)
Medication (13MM/0116)
Infection Control (14IC/0116)
Equality and Inclusion (15EI/0116)

For information on this or other courses please contact:

LEARN CARE EXCEL

Matthews House
21 Thorley Park Road
Bishops Stortford
CM23 3NG

Tel: 07774 880880

info@learncareexcel.co.uk

www.learncareexcel.co.uk

© 2016 Learn Care Excel. ALL RIGHTS RESERVED

Contents

INTRODUCTION 4
A LITTLE BACKGROUND HISTORY 5
    LEGAL SCHEMES TO PROTECT THE VULNERABLE 6
    POVA 6
    SOVA AND THE ISA 6
    DBS CHECKS 7
    MONITORING THE INSTITUTION 7
PART ONE - WHAT IS ABUSE? 8
    TYPES OF ABUSE 9
    PATTERNS OF ABUSE 15
    WHO IS AT RISK OF ABUSE? 16
    WHERE DOES ABUSE TAKE PLACE? 17
    WHO ABUSES? 17
    WHY DOES IT HAPPEN? 18
PART TWO - ROLES AND RESPONSIBILITIES 20
    PERSON CENTRED APPROACH 21
    CARE PLANNING 23
    WORKING TOGETHER 24
    RISK ASSESSMENTS 25
    OBSERVATION 26
    MONITORING 27
    RECORDING INFORMATION 28
    THE VULNERBALE ADULT AS THE ABUSER 30
PART 3 - TAKING ACTION 31
    WHEN ABUSE OCCURS 33
    WHAT TO EXPECT NEXT 35
LEGISLATION AND GUIDANCE 35

INTRODUCTION

When someone is in a position to need care they rely on the carer to provide help and support but in addition they are putting that carer in a "position of trust" whereby the carer is responsible for their basic survival and quality of life because they cannot manage these things for themselves. Unfortunately this leaves the person vulnerable and open to abuse and that is why there are policies and procedures in place to help the carer protect the individual they look after.

Most of us take for granted the ability to be independent and look after ourselves but many are faced with the reality that they can no longer achieve these goals and must rely completely on others. Whether that be someone who is frail and living in a care home, someone who is suffering from a debilitating condition or someone with learning difficulties. Whether that be someone who is permanently living in residential care, someone who visits day centres regularly or someone who receives care in their own home. When someone is unable to look after themselves they are vulnerable to abuse.

This text will look at the way people may be vulnerable and how a carer can help. It is divided into three sections:
- Part 1 - Various forms of abuse, how they can arise and the ways in which someone becomes vulnerable to abuse
- Part 2 - How to work with the client's best interests at heart
- Part 3 - How to recognise signs of abuse and what may be done if someone is being abused

There is also a section at the end of this text that covers details of the legislation that has been put into place to protect the vulnerable.

The subject of safeguarding is not generally discussed openly or comfortably as it can be shocking or upsetting and most people do not believe they or the people they know are capable of such atrocious acts. However, abuse can take many more forms than the dramatic events portrayed in the media and people may perform minor acts of abuse without even realising. Ignorance of the facts can often lead to unintended incidents and believing that it only happens in other places may only prolong the suffering of innocent people unnecessarily. Awareness of the information contained in this course will enable the carer to establish practices that protect the vulnerable and help those who may be suffering abuse for whatever reason.

As with all the texts in this series, information in this course book is aimed at workers in the care industry and discussion will concentrate particularly on the protection of the vulnerable and the elderly in these settings. Although much of this information is transferrable, if you are supporting younger people or people with special needs please consult further texts.

A LITTLE BACKGROUND HISTORY

Before considering the extremely complex issue of abuse it is important to understand that a person's own values, upbringing and perceptions can have a strong influence on what they consider to be abuse and what they do not. A carer must always view a situation from an objective position and take guidance as to what is abuse based on the law of the country in which they live, in this case England and Wales.

When safeguarding someone there is already potential for ethical dilemmas and challenges and remaining objective can be difficult for many reasons, not least they social situation in which they grew up. A care worker's behaviour can be influenced by many things:

- How they themselves were cared for while they were young and vulnerable, for instance, were their parents permissive or strict?
- How they fit into their family unit as they grew older. Was there a lot of communication? Was there interaction with different generations? Was the environment chaotic? Was there tolerance of diversity? Did people have specific roles within the family? And so on.
- How they were educated? This can have a profound impact on their value system.
- How religious, conservative or liberal was their upbringing.
- Their social and economic position.
- Other impactful life experiences.

Equally the person that a carer is looking after will also have their own set of unique influences and behaviours that may be completely different to those of the carer.

In spite of this, however, there are some basic human rights that everyone is entitled to and a special effort must be made to ensure that these are preserved in people who are vulnerable or unable to take care of these themselves.

The Human Rights Act 1998 lists many rights that every human should enjoy and in relation to vulnerable adults, particularly, it offers a starting point for a minimum that a carer must be aiming to achieve. Some of the key rights are listed below:

- Freedom from torture and inhumane or degrading treatment
- Respect for private and family life, home and correspondence
- Freedom of thought, conscience and religion
- Freedom of expression
- Peaceful enjoyment of possessions and protection of property
- The right not to be discriminated against in respect of these rights and freedoms

LEGAL SCHEMES TO PROTECT THE VULNERABLE

It goes without saying that the human rights listed above are just the starting point of what a vulnerable person has the right to expect. In various other Acts, such as the Mental Capacity Act and the Equality Act, many more rights and expectations are also listed. These will be discussed in more detail later in the text but it is important to note that, alongside these Acts, the government has also put into place several schemes to register and monitor people who are at risk of causing harm.

It is important to note that in respect of vulnerable adults there is not a list of at risk people of being harmed (as there is for children) which means that extra vigilance is required on behalf of the carer to identify individuals who are being abused.

POVA

Many of the government's strategies for monitoring people who have caused harm to others have come about as a result of tragic and often shocking events which have led to the extreme maltreatment, and even death, of individuals. For instance, following the conviction of Ian Huntley for the murder of Holly Wells and Jessica Chapman in 2003, the Home Secretary set up the Birchard Inquiry to determine how someone with a history of sexual offences was allowed to be employed as a caretaker in a school, in spite of police checks taking place.

Following the recommendations of this report The Department of Health launched the Protection of Vulnerable Adults scheme in 2004, to list care workers who had harmed vulnerable adults. Since this time all registered care providers are required to carry out a check against the POVA list when hiring for a care position to ensure that they are suitable to work in a care situation. The register is held by the Department of Education and Skills on behalf of the Secretary of State and is managed alongside the Protection of Children Act Scheme.

SOVA AND THE ISA

In further response to the recommendations made in the Birchard Report the POVA scheme was enhanced and streamlined to become the Safeguarding of Vulnerable Groups Act 2006 (SOVA).

Since 2009 employers have the same duty to make referrals as they did under POVA but instead they are sent directly to the Independent Safeguarding Authority (ISA) which is a statutory body established under the SOVA Act to take decisions about who should be barred. It replaced the previous POVA, POCA and List 99 checks. Also the Criminal Records Bureau (CRB) and the ISA merged into the Disclosure and Barring Service (DBS). CRB checks are now called DBS checks.

DBS CHECKS

There are three types of checks that an employer or organisation should run when they are checking the status of an individual:

1. **Standard check** for spent and unspent convictions, cautions, reprimands and final warnings.
2. **Enhanced check** to check all of the above plus additional information held by local police forces that is reasonably considered relevant to the post applied for.
3. **Enhanced with list check** to check 1. and 2. plus a check of the appropriate DBS barred lists.

Ordinarily, employers aren't allowed to ask job applicants about spent convictions, but for positions that require an "enhanced with lists check", such as those who work with vulnerable adults, this rule is waived.

A sample of some of the posts that require a DBS check are listed below[1] but this list is far from exhaustive and further guidance can be given by the DBS.

Providing Health Care
The provision of psychotherapy and counselling to an adult which is related to health care the adult is receiving from, or under the direction or supervision of, a health care professional, is regulated activity, including psychotherapy and telephone counseling.

Providing Personal Care
Anyone who provides an adult with physical assistance with eating or drinking, going to the toilet, washing or bathing, dressing, oral care or care of the skin, hair or nails because of the adult's age, illness or disability, is in regulated activity.

Providing Social Work
The activities of regulated social workers in relation to adults who are clients or potential clients are a regulated activity. These activities include assessing or reviewing the need for health or social care services, and providing ongoing support to clients.

Assistance with general household matters
Anyone who provides day to day assistance to an adult because of their age, illness or disability, where that assistance includes at least one of the following, is in regulated activity: a. managing the person's cash, b. paying the person's bills, or c. shopping on their behalf.

MONITORING THE INSTITUTION

The Health and Social Care Act 2008 introduced a new, single registration system that applies to all health care and adult social care services. The registration system is based on CQCs ongoing assessment of the ability of providers to ensure the quality of people's experiences of the care they receive, including safeguarding and safety.

---

[1] Source: www.gov.uk/government/uploads/system/uploads/attachment_data/file/216900/Regulated-Activity-Adults-Dec-2012.pdf

PART ONE - WHAT IS ABUSE?

A single or repeated act, or lack of appropriate action, occurring within any relationship where there is an expectation of trust which causes harm or distress to a person or violates their human and civil rights.[2]

An incident of abuse can be caused by people's deliberate intention to harm, failure to take the right action or ignorance. It can involve one or a number of people.

Abuse is a violation of an individual's human rights by any other person or persons.[3]

There are countless forms that abuse can take from a deliberate act with the intent of hurting someone to the unintended harm caused to a loved one by someone being over protective. As seen above it can be one incident or a series of incidents but, equally, it can be done to a single person or a whole group of people in the case of institutional abuse. It can be physical, emotional or financial. It can be an act or an omission to act. And it can occur in almost any relationship that a vulnerable person is in from a close family member to a virtual stranger.

When abuse happens it can be devastating with both short and longer term effects on the individual including (but not limited to) lack of confidence, reduced self-esteem and anxiety, withdrawal and depression, insecurity and constant need of approval, and anger, aggression or abusive behaviour to others. It also has the potential to negatively and permanently impact on the person's health, happiness and sense of security.

Whatever the form of abuse, it is imperative that a carer acts with the client's best interests in mind to stop the abuse. People who live in care homes have as much right as anyone else to live their lives free from abuse and neglect. The government has established a variety of measures to support this right and ensure that care services preserve the dignity, independence and well-being of those who use the services.

These have been enshrined into law to enable the government to enforce these principles:
- CRIMINAL LAW – where it is an offence to kill, assault or injure another person, to steal from them or obtain any advantage from them by deception
- HUMAN RIGHTS – protecting a person's right to be free from harm for any reason.

---

[2] Source: Protecting our Future, Report of the Working Group on Elder Abuse, September 2002
[3] Source: No secrets, Dept of Health 2000

TYPES OF ABUSE

Elderly people can be very vulnerable to abuse. This is because, as their mental and physical abilities deteriorate, they become more dependent on others and less able to speak up for themselves.

It is important that policies and procedures exist in every professional care situation and that staff should be trained in recognizing the signs of abuse and how to report incidents of, or suspicions about, abuse taking place.

TYPES OF ABUSE AND SIGNS/SYMPTOMS

1. ***PHYSICAL ABUSE**: deliberately hurting someone or causing physical harm or injury including but not limited to:*
    - Hitting
    - Slapping
    - Pushing
    - Kicking
    - Misuse of restraint

Indicators include:

- Multiple bruising, including black eye, that are un explained or not consistent with the explanation given
- Marks resulting from a kick or a slap
- Cowering and flinching
- Abrasions especially around the neck, wrists and/or ankles
- Scalds, particularly with a well-defined edge which indicates prolonged immersion in hot water
- Hair loss in one area of the scalp which is also sore to the touch
- Frequent minor accidents without seeking medical help
- Unexplained fractures
- Frequent 'hopping' from one G.P to another

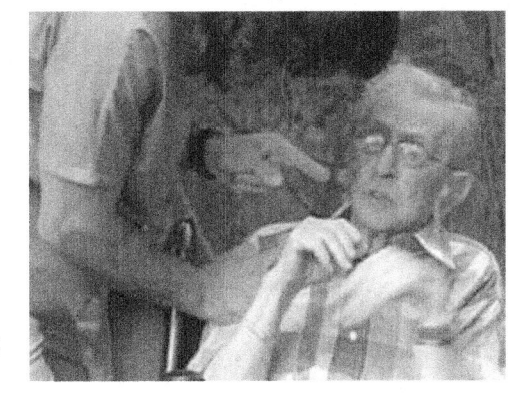

2. **SEXUAL ABUSE:** *any sexual act that was not consented to or which the person felt under pressure to do including rape.*

Indicators include:
- Unusual and unexplained behaviour such as withdrawal, avoiding someone, flinching for no apparent reason
- Difficulty walking
- Soreness, bruising or bleeding around the genital or rectal area
- Urinary tract infections or sexually transmitted disease that do not fit with the medical history
- Recent development of openly sexual behaviour/language including masturbation
- Self-harm
- Irregular or disturbed sleep patterns
- Excessive washing
- Unexplained love bites
- Stained or torn underclothing especially with blood or semen

3. **DISCRIMINATORY ABUSE:** *the intent must be to discriminate. It can take many forms including but not limited to:*
    - Racism, sexism or homophobia, ageism or discrimination against their disability
    - Exclusion based on any of the above
    - Acts or comments intended to cause harm based on any of the above

Indicators include:
- The vulnerable person is subjected to discriminatory comments
- The cultural or religious needs of the person are not respected or met
- The individual complains of comments, exclusions or difficulties due to their race, gender, religion, sexual orientation, age or ability

4. **_PSYCHOLOGICAL AND EMOTIONAL ABUSE:_** _the use of threats or intimidation intended to cause fear or lower self- esteem. It can occur in the following forms:_
    - Abusive language and threats
    - Controlling behaviour including deprivation of contact and isolation from supportive networks
    - Humiliation and blaming
    - Intimidation, bullying, harassment and coercion

Indicators include:
- Anxiety, confusion or general resignation
- Extreme submissiveness or dependency in contrast with known capacity
- Sharp changes in behaviour in the presence of certain persons
- Excessive or inappropriate craving for attention
- Extreme self-abusive behaviour especially self-harm, head banging, hand biting
- Disturbed sleep or tendency to withdraw to a room or bed
- Loss of appetite or eating especially at inappropriate times

5. **_FINANCIAL OR MATERIAL ABUSE:_** _the extortion of money or manipulation in order to gain money or goods through theft, fraud, exploitation, misuse of property, possessions or benefits or undue pressure regarding inheritance or financial transactions_

Indicators include:
- Unexplained or sudden withdrawal of money from accounts
- Contrast between known income or capital and unnecessarily poor living conditions especially where it had developed recently
- Personal possessions of value go missing from the home without satisfactory explanation
- Unexplained or sudden inability to pay bills
- Person responsible for paying bills is apparently not doing so
- Unusual interest of a relative, friend or neighbour in the person's financial assets, particularly if there is little interest in other matters
- Next of kin insists upon informal arrangement to handle finances contrary to advice
- Refusal of care services under pressure from family or other potential beneficiaries
- Unusual purchases unrelated to the known interests of the vulnerable adult e.g. fashionable clothes, expensive make-up, food and holidays

6. ***INSTITUTIONAL ABUSE***: *an organization imposing rigid and insensitive routines; unskilled, intrusive or invasive interventions; or an environment allowing inadequate privacy or physical comfort. This can be seen through collective failing of the organisation to meet care standards, poor attitude or behaviour toward the service users (discrimination, thoughtlessness, stereotyping) or even a failure to ensure the correct safeguards are in place such as training, supervision, management and record keeping.*

Indicators include:
- Lack of care plans
- Contact with the outside not encouraged
- Few visitors or staff insistent on notification before visits are made
- Rigid and fixed 'visiting hours' with no opportunity to individualized arrangements. Visitors are restricted to certain areas. No facilities designed for residents to receive visitors privately
- An unnatural 'clinical' cleanliness with restrictions to ensure this
- An atmosphere which is oppressively quiet or particularly noisy and fractious
- Low staff morale, high turnover or high sickness rate amongst staff
- Complaints from ex-staff or ex-residents
- Staff seem remote from the day to day caring
- Staff lack appropriate skills or engage in bad practice
- Poor or unresponsive complaints system
- Lack of care when dealing with personal clothing, spectacles, hearing aids or teeth
- Strong smell of urine, dirty bed linen
- Residents appear unusually subdued, or regularly retreat into their own room or other areas out of the way of staff
- Clients not allowed flexibility or to express their opinion about meals, bedtimes, routines, outside or extracurricular activities, or even medical procedures
- Lack of respect for personal space or possessions
- Lack of consideration for privacy and dignity, particularly in personal care or contact with friends and family

7. **NEGLECT AND/OR ACTS OF OMMISSION:** *intentionally or unintentionally ignoring medical or physical care needs, including failure to provide appropriate health or social care or to provide the necessities of life such as medication, food, drink or heating.*

Indicators include:
- Poor hygiene and cleanliness of a person who needs assistance with personal care
- Unkempt or unsuitable clothing for the weather conditions
- Untreated physical illness
- Dehydration or weight loss
- Repeated infections
- Repeated unexplained falls/trips
- Pressure sores
- Malnutrition, ulcers and sores due to lack of care for incontinence
- Furnishings, carpeting noticeably shabbier or of poorer quality in their rooms compared with those in other rooms of the house
- Incontinence issues not addressed e.g. odour has developed on clothing or furnishings
- Failure to ensure the taking of medication appropriately
- Inconsistent or reluctant contact with health or social care agencies
- Failure to ensure appropriate privacy and dignity in personal living conditions
- No access to external facilities or access other care services
- Lack of safety equipment being used following recommendation

8. **CHEMICAL ABUSE**; *over-use of medication to control or manage their behaviour.*

Indicators include:
- Constantly appearing drowsy
- Repeated falls
- Low staff / patient ratios or poor management
- Lack of medication reviews
- Use of medical or nursing procedures that are not appropriate e.g. enemas, catheterization

---

Drugs or alcohol misuse, particularly by the carer
This issue is often called "the invisible epidemic" as it is more prevalent than people think, to the point where nurses often attend people who need "reduction programmes" due to an over use of tranquilisers, self-medicated alcohol or pain relief often leading to acute and chronic withdrawal symptoms.

DON'T IGNORE IT!

Every organization should be acting with the best interests of their clients at heart and so should welcome reports of any situation which goes against this. Staff should be made aware that they encourage whistle blowing and will act to restore the best practice if anything is reported, without penalising the person who reported the abuse.

If someone has disclosed to you that they are being abused, or you suspect abuse is taking place, you must inform your line manager.
If that is not possible, contact CQC, social services or the police.

NCEA — 11 Things that Anyone Can Do to Prevent Elder Abuse

1. Learn the **signs of elder abuse and neglect**
2. **Call or visit an elderly loved one** and ask how he or she is doing
3. Provide a respite **break for a caregiver**
4. Ask your bank manager to train tellers on **how to detect elder financial abuse**
5. **Ask your doctor** to ask you and all other senior patients about possible family violence in their lives
6. **Contact your local Adult Protective Services or Long-Term Care Ombudsman** to learn how to support their work helping at-risk elders and adults with disabilities
7. Organize a **"Respect Your Elders" essay or poster contest** in your child's school
8. Ask your religious congregation's leader to **give a talk about elder abuse** at a service or to put a message about elder abuse in the bulletin
9. **Volunteer to be a friendly visitor** to a nursing home resident or to a homebound senior in your neighborhood
10. Send a letter to your local paper, radio or TV station suggesting that they cover **World Elder Abuse Awareness Day** (June 15) or **Grandparents Day** in September
11. Dedicate your **bikeathon/marathon/ other event** to elder mistreatment awareness and prevention

PATTERNS OF ABUSE

In addition to the various types of abuse there are sometimes patterns of abuse that may be identified. Below are some examples:

SERIAL ABUSE
This involves the abuser "grooming" a vulnerable individual or can be in the context of a family or domestic relationship. It is common in instances of sexual or financial abuse and is often involved in cases of domestic violence and controlling behaviour.

OPPORTUNISTIC ABUSE
This usually arises as a result of pressure and stress build up in a relationship, particularly where there is challenging behaviour or high levels of resentment. Most commonly this is a cause of physical abuse.

This can sometimes be because of difficult or challenging behaviour or due to neglecting a person's needs because the carer has difficulties. These could be debt, alcohol or mental health problems

INSTITUTIONAL ABUSE
This abuse can take many forms. Poor care standards, lack of suitable responses to the service user's needs, inflexible routines designed to suit the institution rather than the individual, inadequate staffing levels and poor staff training. It can also be where there are sanctions or punishment (such as withholding food, isolation, unauthorised restraint or over medicating) used against service users who do not comply with the rules of the service. Usually these institutions practice various forms of disempowering or bullying to reduce the self-esteem of the individual or to discourage them from asserting their rights or speaking up for themselves.

SELF ABUSE OR NEGLECT
In these cases it is important to establish the underlying cause of the behaviour as it may not be as a result of abuse from a third person but rather a symptom of difficulties or worries in the person's life or even a medical condition such as dementia.

WHO IS AT RISK OF ABUSE?

Anyone who relies on other people to assist them with some part of their basic daily requirements is at risk of being abused; they are vulnerable as they are not able to look after or speak up for themselves. This includes all sorts of groups of people from babies to migrants but for the purposes of this text we will concentrate on adults in the health and social care system, particularly the elderly who may also have additional issues such as mental, physical or learning difficulties or frailty due to age or illness.

According to the Department of Health's 2000 publication, *No Secrets*[4], a vulnerable adult is someone who, through their condition, is "unable to protect him or herself against significant harm or serious exploitation". The Safeguarding Vulnerable Groups Act 2006[5] goes on to suggest that these people may be, among other things,:
- living in residential accommodation, such as a care home or a residential special school
- living in sheltered housing
- receiving domiciliary care in their own home
- receiving any form of healthcare

So to recap, a vulnerable adult may be someone who has:

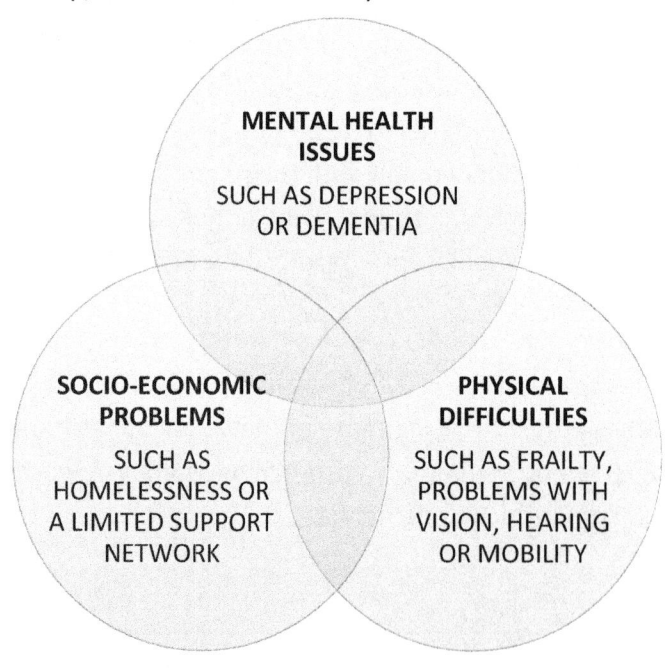

MENTAL HEALTH ISSUES — SUCH AS DEPRESSION OR DEMENTIA

SOCIO-ECONOMIC PROBLEMS — SUCH AS HOMELESSNESS OR A LIMITED SUPPORT NETWORK

PHYSICAL DIFFICULTIES — SUCH AS FRAILTY, PROBLEMS WITH VISION, HEARING OR MOBILITY

As this diagram demonstrates a vulnerable adult can be subject to one two or even all three of the issues that put someone at risk. They can be at risk at any time and this may change as their circumstances change.

---

[4] Source: No Secrets, Dept of health, 2000, https://www.gov.uk/government/publications/nosecrets-guidance-on-protecting-vulnerable-adults-in-care
[5] Source: Safeguarding Vulnerable Groups Act, 2006, http://www.legislation.gov.uk/ukpga/2006/47/section/59

WHERE DOES ABUSE TAKE PLACE?

Abuse can occur anywhere and at any time. It can be sudden and unplanned in which case it can occur anywhere. Alternatively it can be premeditated and executed over a period of time in which case an element of secrecy or privacy is involved. A person could be vulnerable in a hospital, at the doctor's surgery, while out shopping, in a nursing home, while attending a day centre, when they are without a permanent home and even in their own home.

> As part of their care package or enhanced social life some clients will need to visit different places, such as day centres, drop-in community gatherings or the hospital and it is vital that the carer be aware that, even during times when the client is separated from the carer, there is still a duty of care on the carer and they are still responsible for safeguarding the client from harm.

WHO ABUSES?

Abuse against the elderly is usually, although not always, perpetrated by someone that they know. It is also usually, but not always, done by someone with the motivation, opportunity and reason to abuse the person. Abusers can come from any walk of life and be connected to the person via any link and as many recent news reports no one group of people is exempt from being the perpetrator of harm, but almost always they are in a position of trust.

PEOPLE IN A "POSITION OF TRUST"
Partners, children or other relatives
Professional health care staff
Carers
Volunteer workers
Friends or neighbours

> In addition to this list there are also people who manoeuvre themselves into a "position of trust" through a process of "grooming". Older people can be considered to be as vulnerable to this grooming as minors and there are many dedicated networks of people working together to exploit this vulnerability.

At this point it is important to note that abuse against older people is not always deliberate or malicious but instead can result from:
- Poor understanding of an individual's needs and abilities
- Poor understanding of aggression as a form of communication
- Stress through lack of staff or time
- Lack of organizational support and training

In all of these cases, though the abuse is unintentional, it is the fact that the perpetrator is in a position of trust that allows the abuse to occur.

WHY DOES IT HAPPEN?

As can be seen from the text so far, there are many possible reasons for abuse to happen. There can be countless motivations why someone might want to abuse someone. Similarly there are countless reasons why someone might be vulnerable to abuse. Finally, without vigilance there are countless opportunities for abuse to take place. This section will consider why abuse happens in more detail as, through understanding the causes of abuse, a carer will be in the best position possible to prevent it from happening.

Firstly, as hinted at in the paragraph above, there are three factors in any abusive situation; means, motive and opportunity. It is no coincidence that the three key factors in abuse are identical to those of a crime.   REMEMBER: ABUSE IS A CRIME

MEANS: In the case of abuse of a vulnerable adult the "means" is the actual vulnerability of that adult. Without their vulnerability the abuse could not happen. The more dependent someone is on the help of others the more vulnerable they are.

MOTIVE: As previously discussed the motive to abuse someone could be pre-planned or it could be an inappropriate, spur-of-the-moment reaction. People who care for others are in a position of power and have the ability to misuse that power to cause harm.

OPPORTUNITY: If the supportive network or policies and procedures that are designed to protect a person are not operating for whatever reason then a potential abuser will have the opportunity to carry out their abuse.

But perhaps the biggest question that remains unanswered by the above is "Why would someone who is charged with caring for a vulnerable individual become their abuser?"

According to the knowledge set book for Safeguarding Vulnerable Adults there are 7 possible reasons that are known to contribute to someone becoming an abuser:

1. Prolonged stress amongst the care givers or care workers
2. Feelings of resentment and hostility towards the individual
3. Deeply held prejudices and stereotypes
4. Financial dependency on the individual by a child or spouse
5. Unrestricted access to an individual's finances by a child or spouse
6. A limited ability or knowledge in caring for the individual
7. Inadequate monitoring or supervision of a carer or care worker

STRESS

Looking after someone is difficult at the best of times but caring for someone with dementia, say, has many added pressures such as watching a loved one fade away into a stranger or erratic and challenging behaviour. Relationships are put under pressure, tempers fray and the carer can find themselves lashing out.

RESENTMENT AND HOSTILITY

Often the idea of having to look after a parent or spouse is not something that a person may have considered until they find themselves in that position with severe restrictions on their own life as a result. Couple that with the fact that some elderly people can be difficult to look after and resentment can creep into the relationship, even escalating to hostility if they feel that they are not being appreciated or are being treated badly themselves.

PREJUDICE AND STEREOTYPES

This can take the form of generalizations and assumptions that elderly people are a particular way and, for instance, should be treated like babies. Or it can go much deeper and reflect a deep-seated judgement that a carer will make about someone based solely on their religion, race or sexual orientation. The only way to deal with this sort of abuse is through education.

FINANCIAL DEPENDENCY AND FREEDOM OF ACCESS

A carer who has to give up their job, say, to care for a vulnerable person may feel resentment that they now rely on that person for money or resources. It can feel diminishing, particularly if the person was previously very independent.

If the carer is then put into a position of trust to control the vulnerable person's estate the temptation to "help themselves" can be irresistible, especially if they feel they "deserve" it.

POOR SUPPORT OR TRAINING

Without adequate supervision carers will often end up working in isolation meaning that they may adopt poor behaviours or techniques. An informal carer may just be playing out pattern of family violence that existed before the individual became vulnerable. In these cases the best remedy is an adequate training programme and a support network which the carer can go to for help.

Without adequate support the vulnerable person may also become isolated from the support that will help to protect them from abuse. In these cases contact with social services will monitor the situation.

PART TWO - ROLES AND RESPONSIBILITIES

Any person who cares for someone else has a duty of care to safeguard that person. That means they have a moral and legal responsibility to respect the rights of that person. People who are employed as carers are professional and so have a higher duty to protect the vulnerable person from physical, emotional and social harm and abuse at all times.

Agencies whose purpose is to look after and protect people work together by setting up a framework of guidelines to establish the most effective way of preventing abuse and dealing with it when it does occur. The first and most important part of this framework is communication and it is key that the carer understand their role within this framework so that they are able to communicate in the right way with the right people. Family, friends, healthcare professionals, social services, advocates, CQC, the police and even fellow care workers should all work together to ensure a protective net surrounds the vulnerable individual. Working together as a team, sharing procedures and committing to a joint undertaking to protect the vulnerable increases the opportunity for safeguarding.

The second, but no less important, part of the protective framework is sharing concerns. It can be daunting to do so but carers must remember that they have a duty of care to report any abusive behaviour to protect the vulnerable individual. When concerns are shared a proper assessment can be carried out as to the level of risk, allowing appropriate action to be taken.

Anyone can be an abuser, regardless of their status and position. Anyone who is vulnerable can be abused. An environment where "whistle-blowing" is encouraged is the best way to ensure vulnerable people are protected and if this is truly the aim of the care setting the information will be appreciated and acted upon swiftly.

Good framework of safeguarding policies **+** Good communicaion and reporting procedures **=** Good Safeguarding

PERSON CENTRED APPROACH

Over the past 20 years the approach to caring for people has changed significantly. It has moved from one where the service user must adapt to fit with the practices of the care institution to one where the person is at the centre of the care programme and the service must adapt to their needs and wishes.

According to the Government's National Service Framework for Older people it should be the aim of care providers to ensure that older people are treated as individuals and they receive appropriate and timely packages of care which meet their needs as individuals. One of the ways of achieving this is to implement the Person-Centred Care Approach. This involves:

 Listen to the person	 Show the person respect by allowing them to keep their dignity and privacy
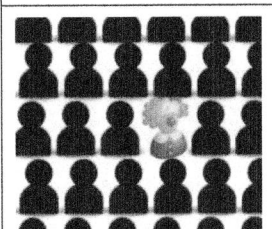 Recognise individual differences and specific needs including cultural and religious differences	Enable the person to make informed choices. Involve them in all decisions about their needs and care 

In terms of safeguarding vulnerable individuals the Person-Centred Approach means ensuring that the individual is free from:

- Neglect or acts of omission, failure to provide care, warmth and treatment
- Harm, or the fear of harm, in the forms of physical, sexual, financial and emotional abuse

Good practice, however, means meeting the needs of the whole person and, in addition to ensuring they feel safe and secure, good safeguarding means that the carer must also consider an individual's cultural, religious and social preferences (such as traditional clothing or special diets they choose) to ensure they do not feel discriminated against. It also means that special attention must be paid to their human rights as they may not be able to insist upon them themselves. The Care Quality Commission (CQC) monitors and protects the rights of people in care settings and these include the right to:

- Privacy and dignity
- A social life
- Good food
- Health and well-being
- Choice and control
- Clean comfortable safe environment

Obviously, in these situations a careful, Person-Centred assessment would need to be carried out. This means:

- A full assessment is carried out prior to any service being offered and reviews are carried out on an ongoing basis to ensure it is possible to safeguard the individual, including the possibility of bullying, reckless behaviour or even self-harm
- Detailed records to show that the individual is fully involved in the assessment process and the language used in the assessment is appropriate to all parties
- Religious and cultural needs are fully understood and met
- The well-being of the individual is actively promoted
- The care plans are laid out in such a way that they may be used as communication, recording and evaluation tools
- Named carers or key workers are matched appropriately to the individual
- Relatives and significant others are made to feel involved and supported

Please see our course book Person-Centred Planning (06PC/0116) for more information.

CARE PLANNING

As part of the Person-Centred Approach it is important to set up a detailed and structured care plan which takes into account an individual's need with regard to their health, personal, social, economic, educational, mental health, ethnic and cultural background.

Setting up a good care plan in this way will help build a person's confidence in themselves as they will feel positive and secure that they are understood physically, socially and emotionally. Building confidence is one of the best ways to counteract the vulnerability that makes people prone to abuse. Carers can help their clients set up an effective plan by:

- Encouraging clients to be independent and to make their own decisions
- Respecting clients as individuals and not behaving in a discriminatory way
- Ensuring that they respect the confidentiality of any information given
- Encouraging clients to participate in their own care planning – agreeing, arranging and managing the services or help needed to support them in living at home, receiving treatment or living in a more supported environment

The development of a care plan takes place in four stages and at each stage there must be thought given to how a person's ability to remain free from abuse is impacted.

Step 1: Assessment
Determine individual's history, current circumstances and needs, agree what care is needed in the future.
Step 2: Implementation
Encourage independence and providing the agreed support.
Step 3: Monitoring
Request and provide feedback, checking if any of the circumstance have changed.
Step 4: Evaluation
Review the feedback and any new information and agreeing new goals.

A good care plan will cater to the individual's care needs and the reasons for providing this care, make note of their goals as well as a time scale for achieving them, and note when and how it will be reviewed. Importantly, though, it will also make a note of times or areas where the individual will require extra safeguarding and make recommendations in this regard. Should the individual set up any "advanced wishes" under the Mental Capacity Act? Should they engage the services of an advocate? Are there any extra measures that can be employed now to reduce the individual's risk? More information on this will be covered in later sections.

Setting up a good care plan in accordance with the above principles will not only help to safeguard the individual but it is also a way of demonstrating that the care provider is fulfilling their duty of care.

WORKING TOGETHER

Implementing the Person-Centred Approach and a properly prepared care plan are only part of the job when it comes to safeguarding an individual. The interactions between people living in care homes and those trained to care for them and those who assist in their care is also a key part of keeping people safe. Recognizing the importance of other healthcare professionals and friends or family is just as important as knowing what carers can do for the client.

Looking after elderly and vulnerable people often involves a multi-disciplinary team who will work together to deliver the best care possible to that person. This means keeping track of all the client's movements and who is coming to see them, when and why. And even when the carer can be sure that the people who are coming in to contact with the vulnerable person are not causing them any harm another important potential abuser is the vulnerable person themselves. For instance, it may be a simple case of refusing to use assistive technologies to get in and out of the bath, risking injury to themselves in this way.

Situations like this need consideration as the duty of care would still apply. Is it better to stop the client from having a bath and give them a bed bath instead or does that impinge on their basic human rights? In this situation having a team to discuss the issue with stops the carer from feeling confused and isolated and the combined experience of the team may come up with a solution that suits everyone. ***Never be afraid of asking for advice from managers or other health care professionals, or even the client's family, when complicated issues such as these arise.***

Below is a list of some of the multi-disciplinary agencies and individuals who work alongside the care team to form the best safeguarding situation for vulnerable adults

- Friends and Relatives
- Local Authorities
- Social Service Authorities
- Care Quality Commission (CQC)
- Care Home Management
- GP and Primary Care staff
- Care Staff
- Police Service
- Independent Mental Capacity Advocates
- Independent Advocates

RISK ASSESSMENTS

Without performing a thorough risk assessment it is impossible to tell were situations of risk might exist. The carer plays a vital role in this assessment as they can assist in identifying ways in which an individual could become at risk of harm or abuse.

When performing a risk assessment the following are some of the points which should be considered:
- Level of communication and understanding of the individual
- Any disability of the individual, particularly those which might increase their vulnerability, such as blindness
- The living arrangements of the individual and how care is provided in those settings
- Any physical risks in their place of residence
- The perception the individual has around their own level of risk
- The awareness the individual has about what abuse is and the ways in which they are vulnerable to it.

It goes without saying that the carer, too, must have an indepth understanding of what constitutes abuse and where it could arise in order to perform an assessment satisfactorily. As already stated everyone has their own unique set of life experiences and influences and they may have different ideas about what abuse is. That is why training in what is required under the CQC is so important.

Following a risk assessment the findings should be noted in a document and included with the care plan so that everyone who gets involved with caring for the individual can be fully advised as to the actions to be taken, and confusion and inconsistence can be avoided. As with all other parts of the care plan the safeguarding assessment should be regularly reviewed.

OBSERVATION

Following the risk assessment the next step in safeguarding an individual is observation. But unlike the risk assessment observation should be carried out on an ongoing basis. That way the carer will get to know the client well and will notice changes in their behaviour or health immediately.

Constant observation also means that the carer may be on hand to prevent or mitigate a sudden or unexpected incident of abuse, including times when they may harm themselves, whether deliberately or accidentally.

One final point to consider is that it may not always be just the service user who is being abused and a carer may witness fellow carers, managers or even family members of the service users being abused. In these instances the same guidelines of reporting the incidents apply.

EFFECTIVE OBSERVATION AIDS EFFECTIVE SAFEGUADING

Some examples of things to observe about the premises:

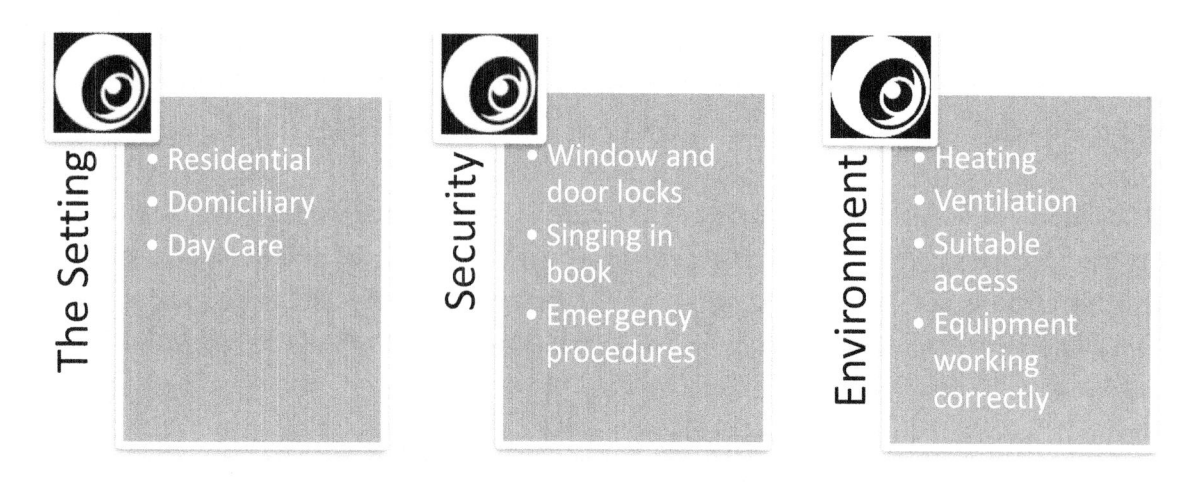

The Setting
- Residential
- Domiciliary
- Day Care

Security
- Window and door locks
- Singing in book
- Emergency procedures

Environment
- Heating
- Ventilation
- Suitable access
- Equipment working correctly

Some examples of things to observe about the person:

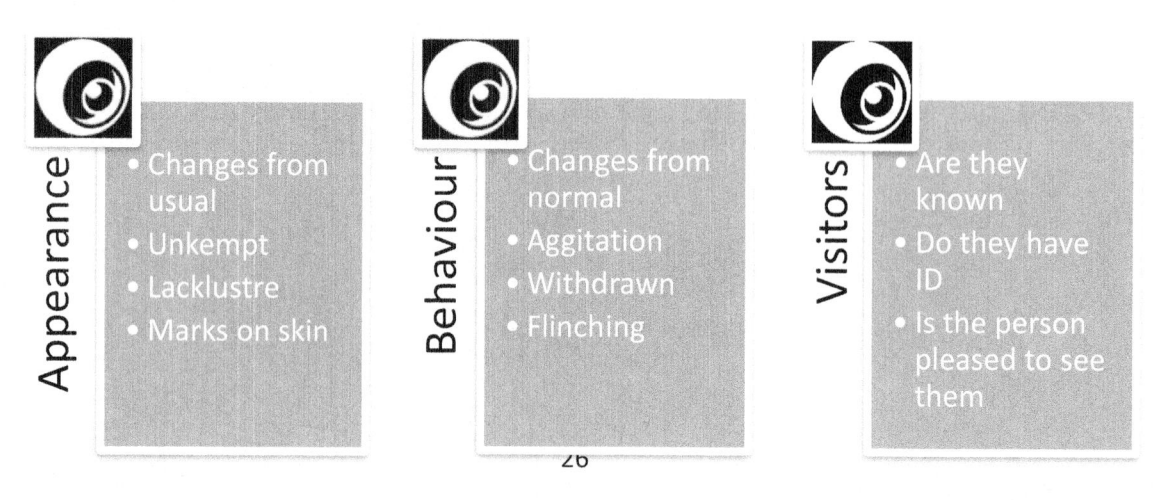

Appearance
- Changes from usual
- Unkempt
- Lacklustre
- Marks on skin

Behaviour
- Changes from normal
- Aggitation
- Withdrawn
- Flinching

Visitors
- Are they known
- Do they have ID
- Is the person pleased to see them

MONITORING

Simply being aware that monitoring is going on can help a service user feel safer and more secure so it is important that they are aware that monitoring is carried out continuously. Ultimately the only people who will object to monitoring for safeguarding purposes are people who wish to cover something up.

Monitoring skills are closely linked to their observational skills in that they require carers to keep a watchful eye on the people in their charge but it is an active, rather than a passive skill. Rather than just generally observing someone, to monitor someone the carer is responding to particular areas of risk highlighted in the care plan specifically; they actively seek to check on a particular thing because it has been pointed out in the care plan as a potential issue. This will apply to situations such as settling in periods, staged self-medication programmes or post-operative care that is detailed in the person's care plan.

It is important to remain unobtrusive when monitoring someone as being too invasive can be upsetting and, rather than increasing the person's sense of security, will have the opposite effect of making them feel mistrustful, meaning that incidents of abuse may not be reported. Equally monitoring should not interfere with other activities. It should be carried out subtly so that, while the person is aware that they are being protected, they do not feel as though they are living in a "police state".

As an example, a client has recently started a "reduction programme" following a period of over medication on pain killers. The risk in this situation is further self-harm but close and obvious monitoring will make the patient feel worse. Ways of monitoring this person subtly can include:
- mentally making a note of how many times a person needs prompting to take their medication and using this to gauge their level of dependence
- ensuring their medication is kept tidy and the records are kept up to date to check that they are taking the medication correctly
- noticing any changes in their behaviour that suggest that medication is being taken incorrectly

EFFECTIVE MONITORING AIDS EFFECTIVE SAFEGUARDING

RECORDING INFORMATION

Without effective and efficient recording of information safeguarding cannot be properly maintained. Recorded information is a key component of good communication and, as has already been seen, communication is one of the most important tools when it comes to safeguarding.

Recording information need not be onerous or time-consuming but it must be recognised as vital to the proper care of a vulnerable person, both in terms of their health and safety.

It can become a part of the carer's daily routine and with practice and clear guidelines the records produced by a carer become an essential part of the care of an individual.

What should be included? Common sense and the care home's policies and procedures will dictate what should be recorded and when but some examples are:
- Notes about the person's medication; what was taken when
- Special requests made by the person
- Any difficulties that arise such as disturbed sleep or problems with personal care
- Any other issues or concerns that the carer has

Where should information be kept? There will be various places where information is kept depending on its purpose and these may include:
- A care file for medical information and so on
- A day book for carer's observations and as a communication tool
- A diary for appointments
- A file of forms and documents.

What happens to the information? Generally information recorded will be a form of communication for all the people involved in a person's care or a way to monitor their progress but it can also be used for:
- Establishing patterns in the person's behaviour
- Recording their preferences
- Reviewing care plans
- And in extreme cases as evidence of abuse

The priority is always to the client and what's right for them

DIFFERENT FORMS AND RECORDINGS

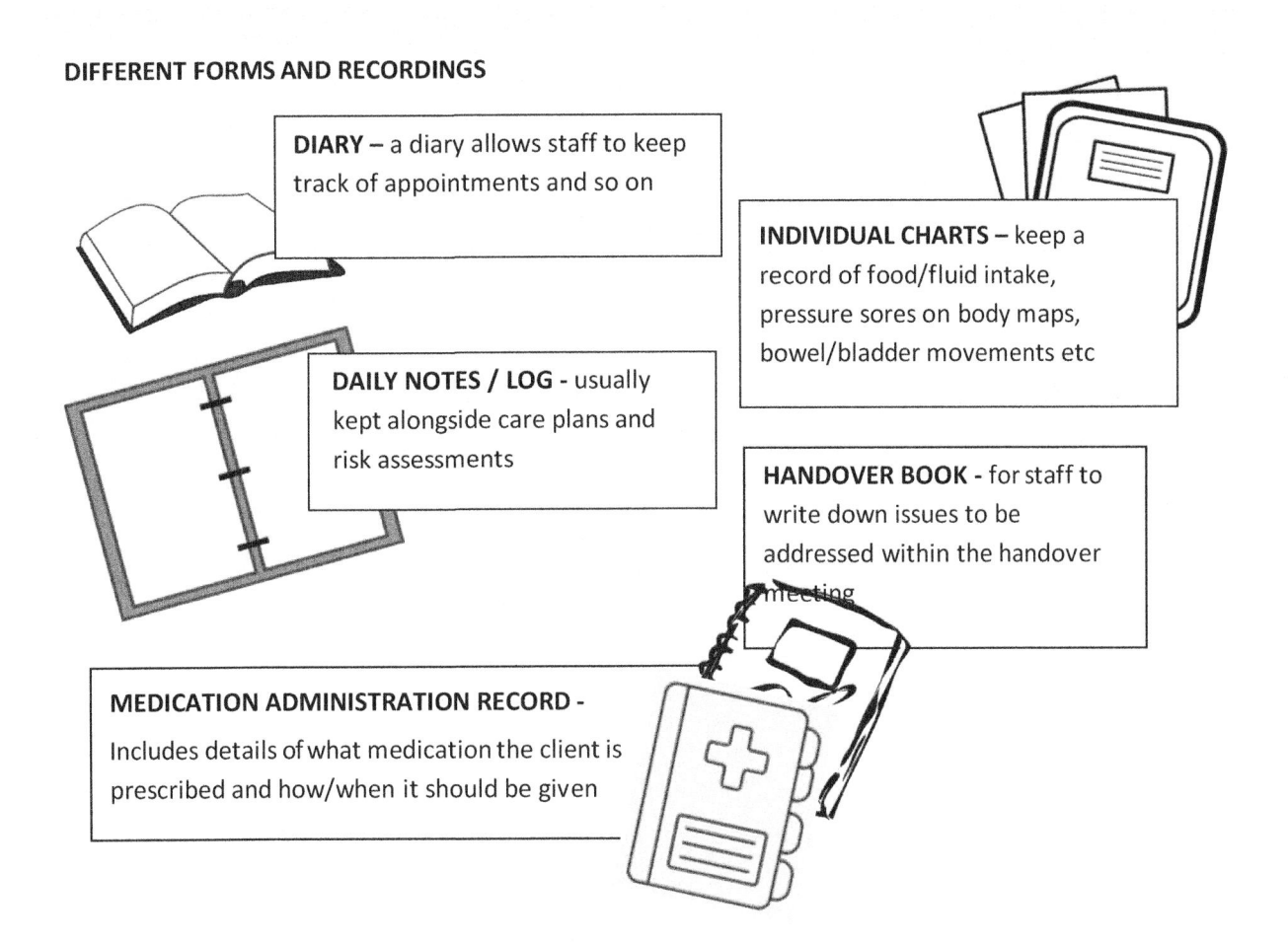

DIARY – a diary allows staff to keep track of appointments and so on

INDIVIDUAL CHARTS – keep a record of food/fluid intake, pressure sores on body maps, bowel/bladder movements etc

DAILY NOTES / LOG - usually kept alongside care plans and risk assessments

HANDOVER BOOK - for staff to write down issues to be addressed within the handover meeting

MEDICATION ADMINISTRATION RECORD - Includes details of what medication the client is prescribed and how/when it should be given

It is vital to follow some basic principles when recording information:

DO
- Write clearly and legibly in pen, not pencil.
- Be factual and objective
- Be accurate, concise and unambiguous
- Write the report as close to the time of the event as possible
- Sign and date the report
- Sign and date any alterations so that it is clear that they were not made at the time of the original report
- Make any required copies

DON'T
- Use unnecessary jargon or abbreviations
- Use meaningless phrases or terms that cannot be understood by others
- Include speculation or assumption
- Use offensive statements
- Include personal opinion unless it has particular relevance to the event

THE VULNERABLE ADULTS AS THE ABUSER

Occasionally the roles are reversed and it is the vulnerable adult who becomes the abuser. This can occur, for instance, when the vulnerable person uses techniques such as manipulation, bullying or controlling behaviour to harm another. As we have pointed out in this book so far, everyone is entitled to their basic human rights and that includes those who care for vulnerable individuals.

Each care home should have a set of policies and procedures that are designed to protect everyone, not just the service users, and if abuse is uncovered, no matter who the perpetrator, these should be followed to stop the abuse and protect the victim.

Wherever possible preventative measures are the best way to approach this situation. Service users should be well assessed as part of their admission process and any suspicions about potential abusive behaviour should be addressed quickly using strategies such as moving the service user to another area or altering their care plan time table.

PART 3 - TAKING ACTION

Witnessing abuse or neglect can be shocking. Having suspicions that abuse or neglect is going on can be troubling. Being told of abuse by the abused person themselves can be distressing. And often knowing what to do in these situations can be difficult.

This section of the text will look at actions that you can take and things that you should do but what is imperative is that you take action. Doing nothing will allow the abuse to carry on causing more harm and a deeper impact on the abused person. It might also encourage the abuser to believe that they can get away with it clearing them to do the same to someone else.

There are four parts to an effective safeguarding policy:

1. PREVENTION – using the techniques mentioned in the previous section, care homes need to prevent abuse from happening at all
2. IDENTIFICATION – where abuse does occur, this needs to be identified quickly and reported in an accurate, timely manner
3. ACTION – once abuse has been identified and reported, homes need to take steps immediately to deal with incident and ensure the safety of their residents
4. PLANNING – homes need to learn from any incidents of abuse and apply those lessons in their planning for the future

Reports of abuse must be handled very carefully to ensure that the best outcome is achieved for the victim while also making sure that there is no unnecessary pursuit of the alleged perpetrator. Poor handling of an abuse claim can lead to the abused individual being in a worse position than before the report was made, members of staff wrongly facing persecution or an actual abuser unsanctioned and more confident to go on to abuse another day.

One way of avoiding these problems is reporting the incident or suspicion to the identified safeguarding manager. There should be one key person who is named and whose responsibility it is to co-ordinate all the agencies that need to be involved in the assessment of the risk of abuse or neglect and in making a protection plan for any individual at risk. This person will also become involved in any reports of abuse and should ensure the process runs smoothly

There may be times, however, when there are barriers to reporting an incident. This could be because the people causing the harm are actually the managers of the care home or there may be inadequate reporting mechanisms in the service. In these circumstances then there are alternative places reports can be made to places that are independent such as the local authority's safeguarding team, CQC or the police. If there is any immediate danger the police should be called right away

Another barrier to the reporting of an incident is the service user may have difficulty with communication. In these cases there should be monitoring forms available that the carer can complete on behalf of the service user.

A final barrier to reporting an incident could be the reluctance on the part of the person who discovered the abuse out of fear of reprisal or dismissal.

It is the responsibility of every care home to ensure that employees are aware that they will be protected in reporting their concerns by The Public Interest Disclosure Act 1998 (PIDA). Under this Act employees who "blow the whistle" about abuse or potential abuse will be safe from "detriment and dismissal".

In fact best practice dictates that managers should welcome whistle blowing as part of their duty of care and this should be included in internal safeguarding policies which as a way of allaying staff concerns.

"All staff working within the care sector should be encouraged to raise concerns about unsafe, abusive or illegal behaviour in the workplace, especially where it threatens those in care. This is an important part of the open culture that all social care services should foster as whistle blowing can play a valuable part in deterring and detecting abuse and for improving standards of care. There is evidence that people who blow the whistle can fear intimidation or being ostracized from their team and it is important that care homes tackle this culture."[6]

An open culture of reporting abuse benefits everyone, except the abuser obviously, and will do more than just protect the person being abused. Effective responses to reports of abuse and clear communication about safeguarding procedures reassure everyone involved in the care of all the individuals being cared for, including their families.

---

[6] Source: CSCI In Focus 'Better Safe than Sorry' 2006

WHEN ABUSE OCCURS

If the carer witnesses something or is given information that causes concern they should:

KEEP CALM
Frightening the individual by being over emotional is not helpful
Keep a level head.
Reassure the victim that it was not their fault and that they were right to speak up

→

MAKE SURE THAT THE PERSON IS SAFE
Are they still in danger or do they need medical assistance?

→

ASSESS THE SITUATION
What can be seen, heard, even smelt?
This may be required for evidence at a later date

↓

EXPLAIN WHAT WILL HAPPEN NEXT
Reassure the person that help will be arranged.
Advise them that this means
CONFIDENTIALITY CANNOT BE PROMISED

←

MAKE A NOTE
Carefully make a note of everything that the person says and everything relevant that has been observed. Be sure to note the time and date also

←

Take time to pay serious attention to what the person is saying and avoid "putting words into their mouth". Ask open ended question to gain as much information

↓

GET HELP AS SOON AS POSSIBLE
Speak to a supervisor, manager, the CQC, local council or the pollice

---

The steps in this table describe what to do immediately when an incident has been reported to or witness by a carer. In conjunction with this there are two more things that a carer must do as part of the reporting process. **Record the incident** effectively and **preserve any evidence.** These are key parts to a report of abuse because they may be necessary if there is to be a prosecution of the abuser but they will also be useful as a learning tool to prevent the same set of events from happening again.

It must be noted that the Care Homes Regulations 2001 require the registered person to inform the commission without delay of:
- The death of any service user
- Any serious injury to a service user
- Any event in the care home that adversely affects the well-being or safety of any service user
- Any allegation of misconduct by the registered person or any person who works at the care home

Any care organization, generally through the manager, must ensure that there is no misuse of power and that an open rule of treating all individuals equally and fairly is put into practice (not just written about in a policy!).

EFFECTIVE RECORDING

Information must recorded:

- Clearly
- Accurately
- Factually
- Timely (written as soon after the event as possible)
- Objectively (avoiding personal opinion as this may hamper future investigation)
- With as much detail as possible (including who said what to whom, where the person making the report was, what action they took and why, and what relationship there was with the abused person. There should also be a body map to record the location of any sings of physical injury)

Details of what the vulnerable person wants to happen next should also be recorded.

Finally the person making the report should sign it, print their name and date and ensure that the record is kept in a safe place.

PRESERVING EVIDENCE

If there is any physical evidence this should be preserved in the following way:

- Ensure written records (notes, letters, bank statements, medication records etc) are kept in a safe place. It can be wise to take copies
- Make a written record of messages (e.g. answer phone) to ensure they are not lost. Include the date and time and sign them and always print your name too. Again keep these in a safe place and make copies as necessary
- Isolate any computers that may have been used, or print off any incriminating pages (e.g. illegal websites). Keep these also in a safe place along with any required copies.
- Don't tidy up, or touch anything, and inform the police if there is any suspicion that there may be forensic evidence.
- In cases of physical or sexual assault encourage the person not to shower or bathe or wash their clothes or bedding if you think they may need a medical examination

Note: The person may not tell you all of the facts on the initial disclosure so do all you can to anticipate what may be needed as evidence and do all you can to preserve it.

WHAT TO EXPECT NEXT

Once an incident has been reported support will be available from other multi-disciplinary agencies such as the local authority or police. The care home manager will also offer support and guidance to the person who has been abused along with any staff members who were involved in the incident in any way. Being involved with a case of abuse can be very distressing but it does occur and carers should take advantage of the support available and not try to cope on their own.

LEGISLATION AND GUIDANCE

A person working within the care industry will find themselves working with many vulnerable people and it can be helpful to understand some of the legislation designed to protect them from danger, harm and abuse.

Older people, people with learning difficulties, physical disabilities or those with mental health issues have rights, laid down in law, including minimum standards of care and several of these are listed below. There is not one overall legal framework for safeguarding vulnerable adults but rather a combination of different parliamentary acts and this have been listed in chronological order for your reference and information. Keep hold of this list so that it may be referred to again at a later date.

HEALTH AND SOCIAL CARE ACT 2012

This act forms an umbrella under which all vulnerable people in whatever care setting are protected. It replaces the previous CARE STANDARDS ACT 2000 which replaced the Registered Homes Act 1984.

The Act follows the National Care Standards Commission (NCSC) which later became the Commission for Social Care Inspection (CSCI) and now is the Care Quality Commission (CQC)

The government introduced National Minimum Standards and established the General Social Care Council (GSCC) for England and the Care Council for Wales. These work towards raising the standards of practice through codes of conduct and practice.

The Act requires that any agency supplying care to a person within their own home (domiciliary) must be registered.

EQUALITY ACT 2010

This act replaced most of the previous Disability Discrimination Act 1995. Under this act, disabled people cannot be discriminated against in respect of:

- Employment
- Education
- Access to goods, facilities and services
- Buying or renting land or property

It also incorporated the 2005 Act which amended or extended existing provisions in the DDA 1995 including;

- Making it unlawful for operators of transport vehicles to discriminate against disabled people
- Making it easier for disabled people to rent property and for tenants to make disability – related applications
- Making sure that private clubs with 25 or more members cannot keep disabled people out, just because they have a disability
- Extending protection to cover people who have HIV, cancer and multiple sclerosis from the moment it is diagnosed
- Ensuring that discrimination law covers all the activities of the public sector
- Requiring public bodies to promote equality of opportunity for disabled people

THE RACIAL AND RELIGIOUS HATRED ACT 2006

Any person who deliberately and intentionally stirs up racial hatred on grounds of religious choice can be convicted under this act. Existing offences in the Public Order Act 1986 legislate against inciting racial hatred. Jews and Sikhs have been deemed by the courts as racial groups and are protected under this legislation, but other groups such as Muslims and Christians are considered to be religious rather than racial groups and have therefore not previously been protected under the law.

MENTAL CAPACITY ACT 2005

This Act was fully implemented in 2007 and replaced part 7 of the Mental Health Act 1983. This also replaced the ENDURING POWER Of ATTORNEY ACT 1985.

Within this act neglect was criminalized i.e. a person accused of neglecting another individual will have broken the law and can be dealt with within the criminal justice system. This act will help and offer guidance to people who can make some decisions about their treatment, and live a mainly independent life, but who may need help with some other aspects of their being – such as being able to live independently but needing help to cook hot meals. This act also incorporates 'advanced decisions' which is when someone with mental capacity decides that they do not want a particular type of treatment if they lack capacity in the future; a doctor must respect this decision.

The act is underpinned by 5 key principles:

- An individual is assumed to be capable unless proven otherwise
- An individual should be supported to make their own decisions
- An individual has the right to make unorthodox decisions
- The individual's best interests must be the focus
- Any intervention should be as unrestrictive as possible

DOMESTIC VIOLENCE, CRIME AND VICTIMS ACT 2004

This act concentrates on legal protection and assistance to victims of domestic violence. It introduced new powers for the police and courts which enables them to deal with offenders quickly and effectively. Under the act:

- It is an offence to breach a non-molestation order
- Common assault is an offence
- Same sex couples who cohabit are covered by the same legal procedures within the act
- Courts can impose restraining orders where the defendant has been acquitted but the court believes the victim is still at risk
- A code of practice for the victims of domestic violence and crime for all criminal justice agencies to practice.

SEXUAL OFFENCES ACT 2003

This is a sensitive area of the law, which until 2003 and not been updated for over a century. It is designed to put victims first and protect everyone from exploitation and abuse including adults, children and vulnerable adults.

The act is non-discriminatory and protects men, women, and all people of other sexual orientation. It clearly and strongly defines what is and is not acceptable. The act reflects the reality of society today.

NATIONAL SERVICE FRAMEWORK FOR OLDER PEOPLE

A National Service Framework (NSF) for older people (aged over 55) was published by the Department of Health in 2001. It is a 10 year framework for improving the health and social care of older people in England. It looks at how best to assess and care for older people, as well as developing an integrated health service between local authorities and independent healthcare providers.

HEALTH ACT 1999

This came into force in 2000 and aims to end the division between health services (funded and provided by the NHS) and social services (run by local councils). The difference between health and social care and which 'illneses' or 'situation' is covered by which agency is very confusing. Regularly hospital beds which are funded by 'health' department are often blocked due to 'social' services not being ready with a care package for them. Ultimately this kind of treatment lacks quality.

'NO SECRETS' DEPARTMENT OF HEALTH GUIDANCE (WHISTLE BLOWING)

The 'no secrets' guidance published in March 2000, did not propose any new legal measures to protect vulnerable adults. The guidance provides a framework within which all responsible organizations can work together to ensure a consistent policy for the protection of vulnerable adults at risk of abuse.

In 2005 the document 'Safeguarding Adults' was published by the Department of Health in partnership with the Commission for Social care Inspection (CSCI) to provide a national framework of standards for good practice and outcomes in adult protection work. Adult protection protocols remain so that multi-agencies continue to work together in sharing information and preparing action plans.

MANAGEMENT OF HEALTH AND SAFETY AT WORK REGULATIONS 1999

This set of regulations require employers to carry out risk assessments, make arrangements to implement necessary measures, appoint competent people and arrange for appropriate information and training. The regulations serve to support the Health and Safety at Work Act 1974.

PUBLIC INTEREST DISCLOSURE ACT 1998 ('Whistle blowers Charter')

This act provides a framework of legal protection which covers the public, private and voluntary sectors. It is intended for individuals who disclose information to expose malpractice and matters of similar concern. Put simply, it protects whistle blowers from victimisation and dismissal.

The scope of the act extends to the raising of "genuine concerns about crime, civil offences, miscarriage of justice, danger to health and safety or the environment and the cover up of any of these".

MODERNISING SOCIAL SERVCES 1998

In 1998 the government published a white paper which sets out the programme for modernizing the social services. It aims to tackle the perceived failures in terms of:

- Protection of vulnerable adults
- Coordination of services between different agencies
- Flexibility of services to meet service users needs
- Clarity over what services are, or should be, provided
- Consistency in standards and levels of service across different areas
- Inefficiency and variation in costs between councils

THE HUMAN RIGHTS ACT 1998

The Human Rights Act 1998 gives further legal effect in the UK to the fundamental rights and freedoms contained in the European Convention on Human Rights. These rights not only impact matters of life and death, they also affect the rights you have in your everyday life: what you can say and do, your beliefs, your right to a fair trial and other similar basic entitlements.

Most rights have limits to ensure that they do not unfairly damage other people's rights. However, certain rights such as the right not to be tortured can never be limited by a court or anybody else. People have the responsibility to respect other people's rights. Basic human rights of lire are:

- the right to life
- freedom from torture and degrading treatment
- freedom from slavery and forced labour
- the right to liberty
- the right to a fair trial
- the right not to be punished for something that wasn't a crime when you did it
- the right to respect for private and family life
- freedom of thought, conscience and religion, and freedom to express your beliefs
- freedom of expression
- freedom of assembly and association
- the right to marry and to start a family
- the right not to be discriminated against in respect of these rights and freedoms
- the right to peaceful enjoyment of your property
- the right to an education
- the right to participate in free elections
- the right not to be subjected to the death penalty

If any of these rights and freedoms are breached, the person has a right to an effective solution in law, even if the breach was by someone in authority, such as police officer.

DATA PROTECTION ACT 1998

This act governs the storage and processing of personal data held in manual records and on computers. Under this act, rights are protected by forcing organizations to follow proper and sound practices, known as data protection principles (DPP).

The data protection Act contains 8 principles which state that all data must be;

1. Processed fairly and lawfully
2. Obtained and used only for specified and lawful purposes
3. Adequate, relevant and not excessive
4. Accurate, and where necessary, kept up to date
5. Kept for no longer than necessary
6. Processed in accordance with the individuals rights
7. Kept secure
8. Transferred only to countries that offer adequate data protection

NHS AND COMMUNITY CARE ACT 1990

Requires social services to assess an individual's needs for living within the community. They should also provide clear procedures for complaints, comments, and registration and inspection requirements. Reviews of a person's ability to contribute should also be taken into consideration.

THE MENTAL HEALTH ACT 1983

Many people receive specialist mental health care and treatment in the community. However, some people can experience severe mental health problems that require admission to hospital for assessment and treatment. People can only be detained if the strict criteria laid down in the Act are met. The person must be suffering from a mental disorder as defined by the Act. An application for assessment or treatment must be supported in writing by two registered medical practitioners. The recommendation must include a statement about why an assessment and/or treatment is necessary, and why other methods of dealing with the patient are not appropriate.

RACE RELATIONS ACT 1976 AND AMMENDMENT 2000, 2003

This act makes race discrimination unlawful in areas such as employment, education, training and the provision of goods, facilities and services. The act applies to discrimination in 3 main groups; direct discrimination, indirect discrimination and victimization.

SEX DISCRIMINATION ACT 1975

No person, whether female, male or transgender can be discriminated against under this act. It covers areas such as employment, education, renting premises and incorporates the term 'victimisation'.

Direct discrimination happens when a person of one gender is treated less favourably on grounds of gender. An example of this would be a female earning less money whilst doing the same job as a male colleague.

Indirect discrimination can occur when a requirement or condition is applied equally to men and women but the proportion of one sex that can satisfy the condition is much smaller than the proportion of the other sex. Unless it can be proven that the condition is essential to the job role, indirect discrimination could take place.

The third type of discrimination covered by the act is victimisation. This occurs when an individual is discriminated against because they have exercised their rights under the act.

The Equal Opportunities Commission was established under the Sex Discrimination Act which works towards the elimination of discrimination to promote equality of opportunity between the sexes and to keep under review the workings of the Equal Pay Act 1970.

THE HEALTH AND SAFETY ACT 1974

Requires the employer and the employee to take responsibility for health and safety whilst carrying out work. The act requires employers to provide a safe working environment and supply any equipment required to carry out the role i.e. personal protective equipment. This act safeguards the older people by ensuring they are not put at risk of harm whilst using the service.

LEARN CARE EXCEL

Matthews House
21 Thorley Park Road
Bishops Stortford
CM23 3NG

Tel: 07774 880880

info@learncareexcel.co.uk
www.learncareexcel.co.uk

Printed in Great Britain
by Amazon